"If there's an empty space, just fill it with a line, that's what I like to do. Even if it's from another show."

- WAITING FOR GUFFMAN

NICK AND NORA GO OFF-BROADWAY

NICK AND NORA GO OFF-BROADWAY

Bambi Everson

NEW YORK

CAUTION: Professionals and amateurs are hereby warned that the play represented in this book is subject to a royalty. It is fully protected under the copyright laws of the United States of America, and of all countries covered by the International Copyright Union (including the Dominion of Canada and the rest of the British Commonwealth), and of all countries covered by the Pan-American Copyright Convention and the Universal Copyright Convention, and of all countries with which the United States has reciprocal copyright relations. All rights, including professional, amateur, motion picture, recitation, lecturing, public reading, radio broadcasting, television, video or sound taping, all other forms of mechanical or electronic reproductions, information storage and retrieval systems and photocopying, and the rights of translation into foreign languages, are strictly reserved. Particular emphasis is laid upon the question of public readings, permission for which must be secured from the Author or their authorized representative. We'll probably say yes, but please ask.

Exceptions are made in the case of brief quotations embodied in critical reviews, educational or scholarly purposes and certain artistic and other noncommercial uses permitted by copyright law. This is a work of fiction. Any resemblance to actual events or persons, living or dead, is entirely coincidental.

All inquiries concerning rights should be sent via email to bambieverson@gmail.com.

For performance of those songs, arrangements, and recordings mentioned in this volume that are protected by copyright, the permission of the copyright owners must be obtained; or other songs and recordings in the public domain substituted.

Copyright © 2020 Bambi Everson

Editing, cover art and layout by Frank Coleman
Published by Everson/Coleman

First Edition: April 2022

All rights reserved.

ISBN: 978-1-7375411-6-5

AUTHOR'S NOTE

I have always loved mysteries, especially whodunits. My father was a film historian with a private collection in our home. When I was a youngster, Dad would often screen a classic mystery, and at the reel change, would ask me who I thought the killer was, and why. Even at 10, I could spot an inconsistency.

"The nurse, because she wore high heels!" "The nun, because she wore lipstick!" "The lawyer, because he couldn't have seen on a foggy night!"

My dad always retained his British poker face, but at the end of the film, I felt his approval. I have strived to gain that approval again, years after his death, with my writing.

After writing THE THIN MAN IN THE CHERRY ORCHARD, I kind of fell in love with the characters, and the actors who played them. I have always loved Nick and Nora, and (SPOILER ALERT) since they took Anya from the previous play to NYC to pursue an acting career, it seemed an obvious choice to build on that.

One of my favorite films is SING AND LIKE IT (1934). Sort of a precursor to BULLETS OVER BROADWAY, it's filled with outdated stereotypes and a few frankly appalling scenes, but mainly wonderful character actors, and pithy, wisecracking, rapid-fire dialogue, typical of the period. It served as an additional inspiration for NICK AND NORA GO OFF-BROADWAY.

COVID-19 derailed this production for two years, but I was finally able to gather the troupe for a staged reading at Emerging Artists Theater in March of 2022. I was fortunate enough to retain my Nick (David Logan Rankin) and Gloria (Wynne Anders), both who have been with me since the very first reading of THIN MAN, back when it was my final project at Empire State College. I am eternally grateful to both of them.

Finding the rest of the cast was a piece of cake, as I'd been exposed to so many wonderful actors through my connections to Emerging Artists Theater, KQ Playwrights, and my mentor, Lynda Crawford.

Our first in-person rehearsal was such a joy, as most of the actors had not been on an actual stage for nearly two years. The cast and director gelled like a perfect English trifle. The cherry on top was our director Aimee Todoroff, who arrived with an abundance of clever ideas, a great understanding of the genre, and a contagious laugh. I usually watch rehearsals in a fetal position, questioning every word I wrote, but this group made everything light, fun, and completely trouble-free. I am grateful to them all.

My wish is that someday I can do these two plays in repertory with this extraordinary cast. Hopefully, you will enjoy reading it as much as I enjoyed writing, and re-writing it. I love hearing from my readers, so please stay in touch. I am easy to find, and very grateful. No mystery there.

Bambi Everson
New York City, April 2022

PRODUCTION HISTORY

The first staged reading of NICK AND NORA GO OFF-BROADWAY was on March 21st, 2022, at Emerging Artists New Works Series at TADA! Theater, 15 West 28th St, New York City.

CAST
(in order of appearance)

STAGE DIRECTIONS & SOUND EFFECTS – David Kaminsky
WAITER – Cameron Bossert
NICK CHARLES – David Logan Rankin*
NORA CHARLES – Elizabeth Bell*
ANYA RANEVSKAYA – Sophie Jones
BRIAN TALBOT – Matthew Corry
CHESTER McNEILL – Gary Ray*
SHELDON STUART – Steven Macarus
GLORIA WRAY – Wynne Anders*
LT. CALLAHAN – Cameron Bossert

* appearing with permission of Actors' Equity Association.

Directed by Aimee Todoroff
An Everson/Coleman Production

Special thanks to Paul Adams at Emerging Artists Theater.

David Kaminsky, Gary Ray, David Logan Rankin, Elizabeth Bell, Wynne Anders, Sophie Jones, Cameron Bossert, Matt Corry, Steve Macarus (l to r). Photo: Frank Coleman.

NICK AND NORA GO OFF BROADWAY
By Bambi Everson
Approximately 100 minutes with one intermission

CHARACTERS:

WAITER (40s) Reformed felon. Respects Nick and Nora. Doubles as LT. CALLAHAN.

NICK CHARLES (40s) - World famous detective. Witty and urbane. Devoted to his wife.

NORA CHARLES (40s) - A charming and witty sophisticate. Independently wealthy and madly in love with her husband.

ANYA RANEVSKAYA (20s) - Formerly Nick and Nora's charge, recently out on her own to pursue her acting career. Enthusiastic, hopeful, naive.

GLORIA WRAY (40s-50s) Ex-movie queen of the Silent era. Her career has been stalled due to scandal, but she is "rising like a Phoenix," or so she thinks.

CHESTER McNEILL (40s) Director of an amateur theater company. Desperate. Arrogant. Passionate about his work.

SHELDON STUART (40's -50s) Longtime actor in the Chester's plays. Jaded.

BRIAN TALBOT (30s) Stage manager extraordinaire. Been with the company for years.

LT. CALLAHAN (40s) A longtime, old school, impatient Irish police officer. Think Pat O'Brien. Has had many run-ins with Nick. There is rivalry, playful competition. Lt. Callahan has been "helped" by Nick before, and might harbor some resentment. Doubles as WAITER.

MAN (40s-50s) Walk-on at end. Doubles as CHESTER.

TIME: 1938.

PLACE: A theater in a church in the West 50s in Manhattan, Nick and Nora's upscale NYC apartment, and a bar.

SYNOPSIS:

In this standalone sequel to THE THIN MAN IN THE CHERRY ORCHARD, Anya convinces Nora to take part in an amateur theater production. As is par for the course, a murder takes place and Nick must solve the crime before opening night.

PRODUCTION NOTES:

Nick and Nora (of "The Thin Man" fame) are the perfect sophisticated couple. They drink a lot but should never appear drunk. Hung over, yes, but never drunk. Their banter with each other is teasing and light hearted, never angry. They speak in the quick, snappy mode of 1940s screwball comedies.

When the actors are in the "play-within-a-play," it is important they show a distinct difference between their character, and their character in the play.

For example, Gloria, a silent movie star, is unaccustomed to acting on a stage. In our first production, she chose to be overly loud and demonstrative.

Sheldon is a mediocre, melodramatic actor, trying his best with the bad material. Maybe his accent is too affected, or too broad.

Nora, so sophisticated and sure of herself in real life, is a fish out of water on stage, and struggles with the material.

In fact, everyone is pretty bad, EXCEPT ANYA, who is a truly good actress even with the awful material.

Have fun with this. It takes a really good actor to portray a bad actor, and our troupe brought so much to the material with their choices. Also consider changing the lighting to distinguish between the two worlds.

In our first reading, the intermission came after Act 1, Scene 3, when Anya is taken away. Conceivably, you could have the intermission after Act 1, Scene 2, with the discovery of the diary, though this would not give Nick and Nora any time to change into pajamas.

ACT 1, SCENE 1

NICK walks into a bar.

WAITER
So good to see you again, Mr. Charles.

NICK
Nice to see you again, Sticky. Things are looking up, I see.

WAITER
Oh, very much so. Thanks to you. Clean as a whistle. Head waiter now. And um... nobody knows about my... you know...

NICK
I'll keep it under my hat.

NICK puts his fingers to his lips and pretends to put something in his hat.

NICK
Two martinis, please. Better make it three. One for the wife.

WAITER
Certainly.

WAITER was already prepared with two martinis, but quickly brings another.

WAITER
Where is Mrs. Charles this evening?

NICK
Oh, she'll be along. She had to take Asta to the vet.

WAITER
Oh, dear. Not ill, I hope?

NICK
I'm afraid he needs the dreaded "snip." Our neighbor's poodle is in the family way. Mrs. Asta and the children are very upset. Mrs. Dumont down the street is livid. Her poodle, Miss Puff, was a show dog. The damage is done, but Mrs. Dumont was quite insistent. Poor Asta. Done in by a pretty... um, face. Happens to the best of us, right, Sticky?

WAITER
No offense, Mr. Charles, but they don't call me Sticky anymore. It's Monsieur Ferdinand, now.

NORA runs in with ASTA on a leash.

NORA
(to unseen management)
Oh, don't worry. He's perfectly well behaved!
(loud dog barking)
Nicky! Nicky! Oh! There you are.

NICK
Hey there, boy! Hello, darling! Asta looks in pretty good spirits, considering. You remember old Sticky– I mean, Monsieur Ferdinand, don't you?

WAITER
It's a pleasure to see you again, Madame.

WAITER takes her hand.

NORA
The last time I gave you my hand, my ring went missing.

NICK
Oh, he's given all that up, my dear. He's a changed man.

NORA
Well then, happy to meet the new you!

ASTA barks. WAITER exits.

NICK
Oh, Asta! I know how you feel.

NORA
Oh, Nicky! You don't know! Miss Puff had her babies this morning.

NICK
Did she now?
(to ASTA)
And how many biscuits a month will you be paying in puppy support? I suppose you'll have to get a job, old pal.

NORA
It's wonderful! All the puppies look exactly like the dachshund across the road. Asta has been spared!

NICK
Atta boy, Asta! You are a one-woman dog, just like your old man.

NORA
And we intend to keep it that way. I need a drink. How many have you had?

NICK
Here? Only one so far. I just got here, myself. Here you are, my darling.

He hands her one drink.

NORA
Well, that's not nearly enough. Ferdinand?

WAITER returns.

NORA
Another round, please. And line up three right here. I like to stay one ahead of my husband.

NICK
Well, I think we all deserve a drink. Ferdinand, a bowl of your finest water for Asta here.

WAITER begins to leave.

NICK
And two more martinis for me. What's good for the goose is a double for the gander.

WAITER exits to get drinks. The two gaze at each other lovingly.

NORA
So, darling, Why are we here? I mean, other than the obvious. Extra olives... mmmmm...

NORA takes one out of his glass and eats it.

NICK
I told you. Anya is meeting us. She said she had news. Maybe her sister and that nice fella are expecting.

NORA
Would that make me an aunt once removed, or a second cousin? Families can get so confusing.

NICK
Especially yours, my dear.

NORA
Now, Nicky... You know that Russian business had nothing to do with MY side of the family. In fact, my cousin Simon has done rather well for

NORA (Cont'd)
himself. His vodka is the biggest Russian export since George
Balanchine. And Anya, dear Anya... after what she went through...

*WAITER returns with a tray full of martinis, a bowl of water, and a piece
of meat for ASTA. He places the drinks in front of them.*

WAITER
I took the liberty of bringing this from the kitchen. Beef tenderloin. The
chef dropped it on the floor.

NICK
Well, Asta, this IS your lucky day!
(Holding up drinks)
To you, Mrs. Charles. And to Asta maintaining his manhood.

NORA
And you, retaining yours. I wonder if I should take up knitting again

NICK
Just not in bed, my love. The last time I almost lost an eye.

ANYA rushes in in a flurry.

ANYA
Nick! Nora! It's been too long.

NORA
Oh, my darling! You look radiant. A new man?

ANYA
Oh, way better than that. I got a job!

NICK
Well, that calls for a celebration. Sit down. Ferdinand– Champagne for
all!

WAITER acknowledges and exits.

ANYA
But I haven't told you what it is!

NORA
Doesn't matter. We are so proud of you!

Takes a drink.

NICK
Darn tootin'.

Takes a drink as well.

ANYA
I got a job... in the theater!

WAITER returns with champagne and glasses with a flourish, pops the cork and pours during the next few lines.

NORA
Oh, wonderful!

NICK
Oh, heavens! It's not one of those burlesque things, is it? Where you dance behind a fan? I saw one last week–

NORA
Did you?...

NICK
Helping out an old friend. Binky Barnes. Someone had walked off with the week's payroll. It's amazing how much a woman can hide in her–

NORA
Nicky!!!

ANYA
No. Nothing like that. It's a legit play. Not Broadway. It's what they call "community theater." A big church on West 54th street. It's close to Broadway! We start rehearsals next week but the best part is...

NICK
To the best part!

He takes another drink.

ANYA
There's a role for you, Nora. The adoptive mother of the ingenue. ME!! Oh, it's Kismet.

NORA
We saw Kismet, didn't we, darling?

NICK
Don't date yourself, my little cabbage leaf. That was 1911.

NORA
We saw the movie, with Loretta Young. She is such a beauty.

ANYA
No, the play is called 'The Regret of the Danbury Lilly." I'm Lilly!

NORA
I'm sure it will be a triumph, but I haven't acted since my debutante ball. I had to pretend I adored my date at my coming out party, when in fact HE was the one who should have been coming out!

NICK
(to NORA)
You are a natural, my love. Grace, glamour and brains. Everything that is missing from today's theater, present company excluded. There must be

NICK (cont'd)
more to life than hobnobbing at cocktail parties and the occasional murder.

NORA
So YOU say.

ANYA
I guess the lead is some big deal.

NICK
Asta is hoping it's Lassie. But if it's not you, or Mrs Charles, I couldn't really give a fig.

ANYA
Gloria Wray.

NICK
Gloria Wray, the old silent movie star?

ANYA
I wouldn't know. That was before my time.

NICK
Gloria Wray. Hot damn! She was something. I always wondered what happened to her.

NORA
Oh, darling. I'm surprised you don't remember. It was such a scandal!

NICK
I do love a good scandal. Not as much as you do, my dear...

ANYA
Scandal?

NORA
Way before your time, lovey. Rumor has it that she killed her third husband when she caught him in a compromising position with her director, who she was .. shall we say, "putting in overtime with."

NICK
Right. They never could prove it, though.

NORA
Because YOU weren't on the case, my darling. The whole world assumed she did him in, but the coroner ruled it a heart attack. So strange. He was 36 and climbed mountains.

NICK
Among other things.

ANYA
Oh, my God!

NICK
What husband is she on now?

NORA
I think it's number six or seven. Anyway, her career came to a complete standstill about 20 years ago.

NICK
Pity. She was very good. I wish I could see more of her.

ANYA
And now you can! Much more. Oh, say you'll join the troupe, Nora! When I told the director you were my legal guardian, he nearly fell off his chair. He follows you in the society pages.

NICK
Oh, that's silly. Directors don't read. Who is this man?

ANYA
His name is Chester McNeill.

NORA
Chet?

NICK
(overlapping)
Chet McNeill? The pretentious blowhard who tried to steal you away from me, lo those many years ago?

NORA
Lucky for you, I broke his heart.

NICK
You broke his chance for a free ride, darling. That chowderhead was only after your money.

NORA
And you weren't?

NICK
Not after our first kiss, my petunia. Your wealth was a mere garnish to your hypnotic allure and vibrant personality. Anya, do you want a steak? Mrs. Charles is picking up the tab. Asta seems to think the tenderloin is slightly underdone, but still viable.

NORA
Yes, dear. Please eat. On an actor's salary, you won't get much chance. Ferdinand?

WAITER appears.

NORA
One of your finest steaks for our thespian, one the chef has managed to keep off the floor, and perhaps a baked potato and broccoli?

ANYA
Sure, if you're sure...

NICK
Asta would have it no other way.

ASTA barks.

ANYA
(to ASTA, petting him)
Well, thank you, Asta. I'll save you the bone. Oh, I wish there was a part for you in this play. Apparently, Mr. McNeill is highly allergic. All our costumes need to be from a pet-free home.

NORA
What a dismal existence. I couldn't imagine, could you, dear?

WAITER
Can I get you anything, Mrs. Charles?

NORA
Oh, thank you, Ferdinand. I am feeling a bit peckish. I'll take a few more olives in my next martini.

WAITER
The chef's special today is a spectacular fettuccini alfredo with salmon. Would you like to sample it?

NORA
I think not, Ferdinand. I'm watching my figure.

NICK
As am I.

NORA
After all, an actress's calling card is how they present themselves.

ANYA
Does that mean you'll do it??

NORA
Things are a bit dull around here since Nicky solved The Case of the Tipsy Taxidermist. Imagine stuffing your mother-in-law and leaving her right by the front window, just to collect her social security checks!

NICK
It wasn't all my doing, dear. Once the raccoon got into the house, it was all over.

NORA
Anyway, that was weeks ago. And Nicky's not doing any more detecting.

NICK
Yes. When Mrs. Charles tells me not to do something, I only do it a few more times. I never say never, because life does have a way of proving us wrong. However, my little lotus blossom, I wonder what your family might think about you taking up with theatricals.

NORA
Well, they've adjusted to me marrying you, darling. I don't think anything will phase them after that.

ANYA
Nora, this will be so much fun!

NORA
Chet McNeill, huh? He might still hold a grudge. I hope he'll have me.

NICK
Here's hoping no one will have you but me.

ANYA
And the world of theater.

NICK
Here's to the loveliest women I know, about to embark on their maiden artistic escapade. Knock 'em dead!

The three raise their glasses as WAITER approaches with a plate for ANYA.

BLACKOUT

ACT 1, SCENE 2

A bare stage in a church basement. Some chairs, a table. In the front row (downstage) is another table with papers, pencils, coffee cups etc. This is where the director sits. At rise, ANYA and SHELDON STUART are having their morning coffee. ANYA is studying her script.

ANYA
(reading from her script)
Father, I can't believe you would betray me like this! My whole life, I thought I was somebody else, but something kept gnawing at me, like a dog with a bone, and I was the bone. You have no idea how painful that has been...
(to SHELDON)
Wait. Sorry... Just this bit here, I know Claudette's not my real mother, but when did she come into the picture? When I was in boarding school, or before?

SHELDON
Oh, honey, don't try to understand it. Just say the lines and try not to bump into the furniture.

ANYA
It's my first professional job. I don't want to disappoint anyone.

SHELDON
Professional? Oh, you sweet young thing. Chester McNeill is a second-rate hack. I have been doing his plays for years. This is another of his melodramatic fiascos in the making. Often his cast outnumbers the audience, and I have done solo pieces.

ANYA
So, why are you...?

SHELDON
What? And give up show business? Chet and I go way back.

ANYA
And Miss Wray.

SHELDON
Yes, Our benefactress. She is so convinced this play will draw D.W. Griffith out of retirement, she put her own money into it. After six husbands, she has plenty of it.

ANYA
Well, maybe... (this will be a hit)

SHELDON
Hope springs eternal for the young. Gloria Wray was in Griffith's first picture. "The Adventures of Dollie," 1908. She was the Gypsy Queen. An exquisite beauty. She has already imagined herself in the remake, "Hello, Dollie." Sad, really. The years have not been kind to her.

NICK and NORA enter.

NICK
Behold, the future of Broadway has arrived!

NORA
Oh, Nicky. Don't be ridiculous. Clearly the star is already on stage.

SHELDON gets up to greet her.

NORA
Oh, Anya, this is so exciting. I am so happy for you.

ANYA and NORA hug. SHELDON clears his throat.

ANYA
Nora, this is Sheldon Stuart. He plays Reginald and your love interest.

SHELDON
(Taking her hand)
Charmed, I'm sure.

NICK
Wait, you don't know where that hand has been.

SHELDON
And you are...?

NORA
My husband, Nick Charles.

SHELDON
Are you in this debacle as well?

NICK
Good heavens, no. The schedule would impede my drinking regimen. But I will be front and center every performance, so no funny business.

SHELDON
With this catastrophe, funny is the last thing you need worry about.

NICK
Where is the rest of the crew?

SHELDON
Our stage manager, Brian, went off to pick up the script for the "newcomer." Gloria must make a grand entrance, separate from our director, even though we all know they have been rehearsing more than her monologue in the wee hours.

ANYA
But, isn't she married?

SHELDON
She is naive, isn't she? All's fair in love and theater, darling.

CHESTER enters.

CHESTER
Greetings, all. I hope you two have gone over your scene. It's first on the agenda today. Could it be? Nora Forrest?

CHESTER hugs NORA. It is slightly awkward.

NORA
You know very well I have been Mrs. Nick Charles for years now, Chet.

CHESTER
Regrettably so.

NORA
Please meet the object of your regret – and my parents'– my husband, Nick.

NICK
Sorry, old man. No hard feelings.

CHESTER
You're not planning on sticking around, are you? I read you were shot in the tabloids.

NICK
Slanderous! The man never came near my tabloids!

NORA
He's given all that up, haven't you dear?

NICK
Of course. I am presently working on a case of cherry vodka, just arrived from the Ranevskya Manor in Russia.

CHESTER
What is taking Brian so long? Late again. This really is inexcusable. As soon as we are all present and accounted for, we shall begin. Nora, the years have been more than kind to you. You have aged like a fine wine.

NICK
Yes. She's good and fruity by now.

SHELDON
Mr. Charles. I do hope you'll make yourself available from time to time. I have an... er... personal matter I'd like your advice on.

BRIAN races in, breathless.

BRIAN
Sorry, Chet. You left your medication again. You're getting forgetful. Second day in a row. I picked it up for you at– never mind.

CHESTER grabs them angrily, pops one in his mouth.

BRIAN
Not on an empty stomach. It could affect your ulcer. Can I get you–

CHESTER
I'm fine.

BRIAN
(feigning enthusiasm, actually nervous)
Wow! Nick Charles. In the flesh. An honor! Pleased to meet you. Big fan.

NICK
You look very familiar.

NICK and NORA exchange a glance. They can't quite place him.

BRIAN
Oh, you sent up my twin brother, Barry. Coupla years back.

NICK
(Apologetic)
Ah...

BRIAN
Oh, no worries, Mr Charles. I couldn't stand the guy. Always causing trouble. Oh, Mrs. Charles, here is your script. I took the liberty of underlining your part.

NORA
Thank you, dear.

NICK
Kindly refrain from taking liberties with my wife. That's my job.

ANYA
Don't pay any attention to him, either of you. His bark is worse than his bite.

NICK
However, I am very effective at barking.
(NICK begins to bark)

GLORIA WRAY enters with a flourish.

GLORIA
Don't tell me there is a dog on the premises. Not when I was forced to leave my little pookiekins at home!

BRIAN rushes over to take her coat and guides her to the stage.

BRIAN
Miss Wray! Welcome! No. Of course, No dogs here. Mr. McNeill is highly allergic.

NICK
I'm afraid that was a rather ungentlemanly way to introduce myself. Nick Charles.

GLORIA
Ah, the famous detective. Your reputation precedes you.

NICK
As does yours. I am a huge fan.

GLORIA
If you tell me your mother used to bring you to my pictures, you are certain to get one of my freshly manicured nails in your eye.

NICK
You look just as I remember you.

GLORIA
There's just a little more of me to remember these days. Chet, is that the new girl?

CHESTER
Ah, yes. This is Anya...

ANYA
Ranevskya.

CHESTER
Well, we'll have to change that. It could never fit on our program, much less a marquee, and this...

NORA
Nora Charles. I am playing Claudette as of this morning. It's a honor.

GLORIA
So, she is the "other woman? Will audiences believe anyone would leave me for her?

SHELDON snorts.

CHESTER
Actually, it was YOU– I mean, Madeline– that left. Reginald only married Claudette so that Lilly would have a mother figure. A temporary caretaker. It just lasted 15 years.

NORA
That is obvious in the script, I am sure.

GLORIA
I will decide what is obvious!

CHESTER
Yes. Now, Mr. Charles, if you will excuse us, we don't want outsiders during our rehearsal process. My technique is way too personal. Brian, have you filled the ice trays?

BRIAN
Do we need more than one? I was going to set the stage.

ANYA
I'll do it.

NICK
And I'll be on my way, then. I smell a huge success... or maybe that's the pub next door. Ta-ta, darlings.

GLORIA
Wait! I want him here.

SHELDON
As do I.

CHESTER
Now, Gloria... Sheldon, really... I must object.

GLORIA
I need someone to keep an eye on things. Someone who knows my work and will be objective. Besides, I have a private matter to discuss with Mr. Charles. You don't mind sharing your husband, do you, Nora?

NORA
It wouldn't be the first time.

GLORIA beckons to NICK.

GLORIA
May I bend your ear for a moment, Mr. Charles?

CHESTER
Now? We are on company time, Gloria.

GLORIA
I AM the company!

CHESTER
Yes, of course. Brian, Miss Wray needs a moment.

BRIAN
We are running behind as it is.

CHESTER
What Miss Wray wants, Miss Wray gets. You should have figured that out by now. Tell everyone their coffee break came early today.

BRIAN
Clear the stage, everyone.

Everyone exits.

CHESTER
Go ahead, Gloria, What is TIME, anyway? Just a clock some sucker winds. Mr. Charles, she's all yours, but do try and keep it brief.

NICK
Certainly, step into my office. After you, Miss Wray.

NICK motions to a seat in the "audience," or alternately steps back onstage, some place where there are two chairs and a modicum of privacy.

NICK
Would you care for a snifter?

GLORIA
I gave up drinking on the job years ago.

NICK
When I read about the evils of alcohol, I gave up reading.

NORA rushes up.

NORA
Oh, please let me help! I love helping.

NICK
Of course you can, my petunia.

Hands her his flask.

NICK
I am in desperate need of a refill.

NORA
But Nicky, I... Oh, fine!

NORA stomps off.

NICK
Now, Miss Wray, how may I be of service to you?

GLORIA
Can you be discreet, Mr. Charles?

NICK
I find nothing is as burdensome as a secret. Yours are safe with me.

GLORIA
It's a delicate matter. I keep a diary.

NICK
I thought only good girls kept diaries. Naughty girls don't have the time.

GLORIA
This is no laughing matter, Mr. Charles. That diary has some... shall we say, indiscretions that I don't want to become public. Not now, when I am reviving my career. There is information... if it came to light... the police...

NICK
So, pardon the obvious, but why keep it, then?

GLORIA
I kept it to set the record straight. For the future... but it's missing! Stolen! My suite was ransacked two nights ago. I called security right away. It seemed nothing was taken at first glance, no jewels, no money. My darling pookiekins was locked in the linen cupboard. Management asked if thieves might be looking for something specific. Then, it hit me. The diary. But of course, I couldn't tell the police.

NICK
Naturally.

GLORIA
Yesterday, this arrived by messenger. They want $5,000 in cash or they'll go public. What do you make of this?

GLORIA pulls out a small paper with cut out letters, and hands it to NICK.

NICK
I could make a teeny tiny hat, but that's not too helpful. Ah! Obviously, someone keeps all their TIME magazines. I recognize the letters from the Sept 12th cover. Who might benefit from this information?

GLORIA
Everyone. Anyone. My story was the scandal of the decade. But to be honest, Mr. Charles, I think it's Chester.

NICK
Our Chet?

GLORIA
Keep this on the QT, Mr. Charles, but we are... involved.

NICK
(mocking shock)
No!

GLORIA
It's true. And he has had... access. My present husband is in Europe right now and... well, a woman has needs.

NICK
And means. But you are already financing this production. What possible motive could Mr. McNeill have for...

GLORIA
I don't know. I can't prove it. That's why I need you, Mr. Charles. I've seen how you trip people up. I am a very giving, but surprisingly naive, woman. Many men have taken advantage of that. Hedda Hopper would give her entire hat collection for a story like this. Chet is broke. $5,000 could finance his next five plays.

NORA returns with NICK's full flask.

NORA
Here, darling, The bartender says you have been in there so often, he's naming a drink after you. A gumshoe gimlet. Cheapest one in the joint. What did I miss?

NICK
Hats, my cherry blossom. We have been discussing hats.

NORA
Without me? How could you?
(to NICK)
Next time I see you, remind me not to talk to you.

CHESTER and BRIAN return, clearing their throats.

CHESTER
Ah, if only time could stand still, but it can't. Gloria, my dear, have you concluded your business?

GLORIA
For the time being.

GLORIA looks at NICK who zips his lip and tosses the key.

CHESTER
Then we can begin. Brian?

BRIAN
Ok, everyone. Back to work. Who's got the prop?

ANYA
The ice cubes were already filled. But I filled the liquor bottles with tea.

NICK
Good heavens, the atrocities you actors must endure. Fortunately, I brought my own.

NICK pulls out a flask and takes a drink.

NICK
On with the show!

CHESTER
This is my domain, Mr. Charles. If you must remain, kindly sit in the audience. As far back as you can manage. And Brian, where are those ice cubes?

BRIAN
Coming, sir.
(To ANYA)
We must make sure there are enough. Mr. McNeill chews ice cubes like a madman. He has Pagophagia. A strange affliction caused by an iron deficiency. I am shocked he doesn't chew nails. But don't let his manner dissuade you. He isn't all bad.

SHELDON
Just mostly bad.

BRIAN returns with ice cubes in a bowl which CHESTER crunches continuously.

CHESTER
Actors, we will start today with scene 5. Madeline's entrance. Places, everyone!

GLORIA sweeps on stage with grandeur.

GLORIA
Darling, don't you think I should enter from upstage right?

CHESTER
But the front door is over here.

GLORIA
Yes, but I will have changed my outfit, and it gives the audience more of a chance to see me.

CHESTER
Of course. That makes perfect sense.

SHELDON
Is she coming in through the window like Peter Pan?

ANYA
Maybe she's coming in through the garden?

BRIAN
Yes. Maybe there's a path. Maybe she picked some roses along the way. She could come in with them for Lilly.

CHESTER
Not real ones. I'm allergic. But fine. That could work.

CHESTER takes GLORIA's hand and leads her to her exit. He stops and begins to sneeze.

CHESTER
Gloria, darling, I did ask you not to wear clothes that your mongrel has molted on.

GLORIA
Pookie is utterly obedient, unlike some I could mention. And my dresser took the utmost care in brushing me off this morning.

NORA
Oh dear, I hope it's not us. You see our Asta does like to sit on our laps during breakfast. Nicky, darling, would you mind...

NICK
I would do anything for you, my peach, but I shall not sit on that man's lap. Besides, my suit came back from the dry cleaners yesterday. I didn't put it on 'til after breakfast.

CHESTER
Do I need to make this announcement again? No flowers on set, No perfumes, ladies. No pet hair, and absolutely no nuts on stage.

SHELDON
That last one will be hard to accomplish.

BRIAN
Mr. McNeill has a severe peanut allergy. He is afflicted with F-PIE.

ANYA
How sad. I love a good pie.

BRIAN
F-PIE. Food Protein Induced Enterocolitis. It causes low blood pressure and severe body temperature changes. Another reason for the ice.

CHESTER
Can we get on with things, please?

ANYA
(quietly to SHELDON)
Goodness, is there anything Mr. McNeill isn't afflicted with?

SHELDON
Yes. Humility.

CHESTER
Madeline enters from upstage right.

GLORIA
(as Madeline)
I have returned.

SHELDON
(under his breath to NORA)
Through the kitchen window, apparently.

NORA
(to SHELDON)
Shhhhh!

SHELDON
(as Reginald)
Madeline. I never expected. Oh dear, I am not prepared.

ANYA as Lilly enters.

ANYA
(as Lilly)
I wasn't aware we had company. Shall I make tea?

NORA
(as Claudette)
Reginald?

GLORIA
(as Madeline)
Well, I must say, this was not the welcome I expected. Didn't you receive my telegram?

SHELDON
(as Reginald)
What telegram?

NORA
(as Claudette)
Oh, my goodness! We were on our way to the market when we ran into Bobby...

ANYA
(overlapping)
The telegraph boy. He almost got hit by the milk truck.

NORA
Yes. Dear Lilly had to soothe the horse, while I calmed Bobby's nerves.

ANYA
The telegram... It's still in your pocket.

NORA
(pulling the telegram from her apron pocket)
I'm so sorry, darling...

GLORIA
(as Madeline, wildly overacting)
DARLING? Don't tell me that SHE–

CHESTER
Gloria, let's try to remember that your silent movie days are behind you. Let's try to be creative, not imitative.

GLORIA
This is what my public expects. This face was the voice of silent film. The world was a smaller place then. I brought life to a 40 foot screen, and the world was mad for me. I am not Edna Mae Oliver, for fuck's sake. I was a goddess

SHELDON
(to ANYA)
Was being the operative word.

ANYA
Shh! I think she's elegant. I've never met a real film star before.

CHESTER
(to GLORIA)
Yes, of course, but let's not throw it all out there on the first line. Let the audience savor the sight of you for a bit.

GLORIA
Yes. I see your point, darling. I just got carried away.

SHELDON
(to others)
Not far enough, sadly.

ANYA and NORA shush him. CHESTER grabs some ice and starts madly chewing it. He does this often throughout the scene. GLORIA sweeps majestically across the stage.

ANYA
(to SHELDON)
She really is regal. Did she ever win an Academy Award?

SHELDON
Shhh!

GLORIA
(turning dramatically)
Academy Award? Child, I was a star before there WERE such trifling things as Academy awards. If the Academy really took things seriously, they would give awards to an actor who was brilliant in a bad film. Now, THAT is the true test of an actor. If that was the case, I would have a truckload. But NO! Nowadays, if you play a character with a defect, a maniac, a loony, they just hand you an award. No chance for a woman of class and distinction. I am certainly not waiting around 'til they give me some pathetic honorary deathbed award, because they were too stupid or guilty to recognize me in my prime. But this play... This play will remind

GLORIA (cont'd)
the world what I am made of. And Mr. Griffith will know the world wants me back. We will return triumphantly to the silver screen, together. Better than ever!

CHESTER
(crunching his ice madly)
But Gloria, darling, We must remember, the theater is different from film. There are no cameras coming in for your close up. You must act it so the people in the back row can see and hear it as much as the people in the front row. But we must not overact. We have words to help us now.

GLORIA
I hate those naturalistic actors... mumbling at each other. I shall be seen and heard as I was meant to be.

NORA
(to SHELDON)
Chester's crunching... It's so unsettling.

CHESTER
Of course. You are, and have always been, perfect. Just as you are. Moving on, everyone! We'll take it from Madeline's line, "Well, I'm back."

GLORIA
Can you hear me all right from where you are, Mr. Charles?

NICK
Absolutely golden, my dear. Your voice is a martini to my soul.

GLORIA
At least someone appreciates me. Where am I standing? I think center. Would you all mind scooting back a little?

SHELDON rolls his eyes and grumbles. Other actors give GLORIA center stage.

GLORIA
(as Madeline)
Well, I'm back. Lilly, we must do something about your hair. Luckily, we have lots of time.

ANYA
(as Lilly)
Claudette always does my...

SHELDON
(as Reginald)
Lilly, brace yourself. This is your mother.

ANYA
(as Lilly)
You told me she was dead.

SHELDON
(as Reginald)
She was dead... to me.

GLORIA
(as Madeline)
Dead? I was touring Europe with Ibsen.

SHELDON
(aside, to ANYA)
Madeline must be ages old. Ibsen died in 1906.

GLORIA
Ahem! Please refrain from side conversations during my monologue. It's very distracting. Now, where was I? Oh, yes.
(as Madeline)
Who do you think paid for your years at boarding school Lilly? This house, the gardener and cook. Surely, you don't think your father could have maintained this luxurious lifestyle on his paltry professor salary, do you?

SHELDON
(as Reginald)
15 years, Madeline. In 15 years, you couldn't have sent a postcard? A Christmas present? Lilly grew up without a mother.

NORA
(as Claudette)
Well, not exactly.

GLORIA
(as Madeline, starting to overact again)
And whom might you be? Not the new Mrs. Danbury, I hope. Reginald and I never divorced, you know. Bigamy is still a criminal offense, is it not?

NORA
(As Claudette)
I knew he was married, so we did not speak of love, but darling Lilly, I have always loved you like a daughter. You were the anchor that held me here. Despite your father's rejection. Despite the fact that he never knew that I loved him for the man he is, not the man the town pitied, because he was abandoned and left to raise an infant on his own.

GLORIA
(to Chester)
I am not sure about those lines, Chet dear. They don't portray me in a very nice light. Her last ones I hate. Her others I merely dislike.

CHESTER
If you would, Gloria...

GLORIA
We will discuss this further, but now...

GLORIA sighs, rolls her eyes, and then goes back into character.

GLORIA
(as Madeline)
I appreciate you standing in. My career would have suffered if it got out that I left my husband and child, or even that I had one. The world saw me as an goddess, not a wife. Certainly not a mother. I couldn't chance my past coming to light, but that's all over now, my precious Lilly. You are old enough now to pass as my confidant, my Girl Friday. We shall travel to Paris together. You haven't lived until you have tasted these tiny strawberries that grow only in the south of France. Oh darling, we will have so much fun!

ANYA
(as Lilly)
As your traveling companion? Your attendant?

NORA
(as Claudette)
Reginald, are you going to respond to this?

ANYA
(As Lilly)
I think I shall speak for myself. Miss Madeline, you may have given birth to me, but you are not my mother. A mother tucks you into bed at night and reads you the same story, even though she's sick to death of it. A mother picks the raisins out of my cinnamon bread, because Father likes raisins, but she knows I don't. Claudette did that. A mother shows her love with actions, not dollars. Father, how could you betray me like this? My whole life, I thought I was somebody else, but something kept gnawing at me...like a dog with a bone, and I was the bone.

GLORIA
Oh, really, Chet, do we really need this long diatribe from the child? We can certainly cut all this extraneous information about Claudette. She's a minor character. Who is going to care?

CHESTER
Well, the playwright for one.

GLORIA
Well, I think I should help him with his thinking. Who is this idiot?

CHESTER
This idiot is me! And the lines stay. I do not write minor characters. This is an ensemble piece.

GLORIA
(to NORA)
Yes. We are all made the same, though some of us more than others.

NORA
(Getting ready to take a swing at her)
Nicky?

NICK
(From the audience)
Your patience will achieve more than your force, my dove. Do you need a little tipple to unruffle those feathers?

NORA
I believe I do.

CHESTER
We are all teetotalers in this theater.

NORA
Now I know why mother said acting was a ridiculous profession.

CHESTER
Let's take five, everyone. Brian! Get me some more ice.

BRIAN
On it.

CHESTER
And more Tea!

ANYA
I'll get it.

BRIAN
Back in five, everyone.

ANYA
Thank you, five.

Everyone stares at her.

BRIAN
What is that?

ANYA
Just a polite way to tell you I heard you, and I know it's five minutes, and I won't be late getting back.

BRIAN
Interesting concept. Mind if I use it?

ANYA
Be my guest.

CHESTER
Splendid everyone. I'd like us to take a moment to thank our benefactress, who is sharing not only her great gifts but her checkbook, to see this production come to light. Gloria, we are honored and privileged to have you on board.

CHESTER, ANYA and NORA clap while GLORIA humbly bows. SHELDON and BRIAN look annoyed and clap unenthusiastically.

SHELDON
(Softly, to no one in particular)
All hail our brown-nosed director.

CHESTER
I have big plans. I have an artistic vision that goes beyond this theater, beyond this production. I see obstacles merely as stepping stones to greatness. When there is magic and money, we have theater! In Gloria, we have both. Gloria, would you like to add anything?

GLORIA
Actually, I would Chet. I know you all are probably feeling intimidated working with a great star like me.

SHELDON snorts.

GLORIA
We of the theater live apart from the outside world, but I assure you, I will not let you, the little people, or my public, down. The papers have said this is my comeback, but the thing is, I was never gone!

SHELDON
(softly to Anya)
I think she's rehearsing her speech for Walter Winchell's column.

GLORIA
(getting angrier)
There are incidents in my life I wish would go away. Things we will not talk about here, or ever This theater is my new home. Here is where I belong. Where my story can resume unfettered by rumor and innuendo. You are my new family. Family must stick together at all cost. Trust is fragile, and must be earned. Once broken, it is not easily repaired. And in that vein, Mr. Charles here has something to say.

NICK
I do?

CHESTER
Must you?

NORA
Oh, he must. He must.

NICK
I am a man of few words when I am sober, Luckily, that is rarely the case. It has come to my attention that someone here is in possession of something of someone else's. If that someone returns said something to someone, or to me, privately perhaps, that someone will avoid the hospitality provided by our local police force. If not, that someone is going to find that something might put someone in somewhat of a pickle.

BRIAN
What are you talking about?

NORA
Go on, dear. Who has the something that someone knows something about?

SHELDON
(pointing at CHESTER)
He knows.

CHESTER
Knows what? I have no idea what you are spewing here, Mr. Charles.

NICK
I am not pointing the finger at anyone. My hands are full.

He has a drink in one hand and NORA's hand in the other.

GLORIA
I simply can't be pouring my heart and soul out on stage with people I can't trust.

ANYA
(to NORA)
What's going on?

NORA
Don't worry. Nicky has this all under control. He's so handsome when he's interrogating people.

SHELDON
I don't know how you knew about this, Mr. Charles, but I am glad it's out in the open. Blackmail is so ugly.

GLORIA
Blackmail!?

NICK
How did you know it was blackmail, Mr. Stuart?

SHELDON
You mean this isn't about me?

BRIAN
Typical. Every actor always thinks everything is about them.

NICK
A secret's worth depends on the people you are keeping it from.

SHELDON
I must speak with you alone, Mr. Charles. NOW!

BRIAN
Oh, for the love of Pete. So many theatrics.

CHESTER
Everybody take 15. I'd like to get this play off the ground while Roosevelt is still in office, if nobody minds. Actors... God, how I hate them. More drama off stage than on. Next show, I swear I'm using puppets and mimes!

BRIAN
15, everyone!

ANYA
Thank you, 15.

GLORIA
That child is way too chipper.

BRIAN
It's early in the rehearsal period. She'll wise up.

Everyone walks off leaving CHESTER sitting at his desk chomping his ice and NICK and NORA on stage with SHELDON.

SHELDON
Mr. Charles, this is all quite disturbing. I...
(looks at NORA)

NORA
Are you going to start discussing hats again?

NICK
My wife is very insightful. Would you mind?

SHELDON
What does it matter now? I just announced it to everyone. I got a letter.

SHELDON hands a letter to NICK. Another cut-out letter.

NICK
The mailman must be working overtime. Here, darling. You do the honors.

NORA
(reading)
"I know who you are and what you did." Well, that's cryptic. What do you think it means?

SHELDON
It's got to be from Chester. You see, Mr. Charles, I haven't always been Sheldon Stuart. I've worked with Chet all these years despite the fact that his plays are really awful because... well, he pays me in cash. Off the books. No IDs to check. He must have found out my real identity. That cad. Look at him, just sitting there at his desk, silently. Knowing I am talking to you. What a scoundrel. I have a good mind to–

NICK
Wait. Did you hear that?

NORA
What?

NICK
The quiet. The man has been chewing ice all damn day. Maybe he's eavesdropping. It's all right, Mr. McNeill! All the dirty laundry is being aired now.

BRIAN enters with more tea and ice.

BRIAN
The actors are running lines in the dressing room, but I think maybe... Chet? Chet? Oh My God!! Mr. Charles! Come quickly!

NICK, NORA and SHELDON run over to him. NICK turns his swivel chair around. CHESTER does not move.

NICK
I'm not a doctor, but I'll bet you dollars to donuts, this man is dead. Either that, or my watch has stopped.

BRIAN wails and throws his body on him.

BRIAN
No! No! Somebody help him! Maybe there is something in his throat!

BRIAN tilts CHESTER's head back and presses his chest.

BRIAN
Help! Somebody! Please help!

NICK
Stand back, please.

The rest of the cast has entered hearing the screams, and panic has set in. Everyone is screaming.

NICK
Nora, run next door to the bar and tell the operator we need help here. Then get Lieutenant Callahan here.

NORA rushes off.

GLORIA
Oh, Chet! My dear Chet... I wonder if all this stress was just too much for him. His cholesterol was higher than our production budget.

NICK
(To BRIAN)
What are you doing?

BRIAN
His glass! There is something in it.

NICK
Touch nothing.

NICK goes over to look.

NICK
It appears to be... a PEANUT!

Everyone gasps!

BRIAN
(to ANYA)
YOU!! You gave him the tea!

ANYA
(teary)
But I... I wouldn't... I couldn't... The bottle was in the refrigerator. I only...

NICK
Let's not jump to conclusions here. We don't know how he died. Please bring me a blanket or something.

ANYA runs backstage and comes back with a ridiculous colored coat.

ANYA
This is all I could find.

NICK places the colored coat over the sitting corpse. They all stare.

NICK
Whoever said theater was a dying art form spoke the truth.

GLORIA
(touching CHESTER's chest)
"Good-night, sweet prince; And flights of angels sing thee to thy rest." Wait! There is something here.

ANYA
I hope it's a heartbeat.

NICK
(pulling out a handkerchief)
Allow me.

NICK goes to the body. When he takes the blanket off, there is a gasp and others turn away. NICK pulls a book from CHESTER's front pocket.

GLORIA
My diary!

BLACKOUT

ACT 1, SCENE 3

The actors are still gathered in the theater. The body has been removed. LT. CALLAHAN is on the scene and taking notes.

LT. CALLAHAN
What a surprise, and yet not a surprise, to see you here, Nick. You do have a knack for being in the wrong place at the wrong time.

NICK
Just lucky, I guess.

LT. CALLAHAN
(to NORA)
A lot of things happen to happen every place your husband goes. Do you ever think about that?

NORA
Never a dull moment. But Nicky has an alibi for every moment since I married him, don't you, dear?

LT. CALLAHAN
When Mrs. Charles phoned me, I assumed you were working a case. What's your angle, Nick? Who's your client this time?

NICK
No one. I am here merely as a patron of the arts.

LT. CALLAHAN
Hmmm. I see. And you were all here at the time of the deceased's... death?

NICK
Well, the Mrs., Sheldon, and I were over there. Everyone else was scattered backstage.

GLORIA
I was rehearsing my lines in the powder room. I like the acoustics.

LT. CALLAHAN
Miss Wray, let me just say, I saw "The Lady in the Windmill" a dozen times. You were magnificent.

GLORIA
Thank you. Would you like an autograph?

LT. CALLAHAN
Much obliged.

LT. CALLAHAN hands her his note pad.

LT. CALLAHAN
Make it out to Patty with an "IE." My wife. She sees all your pictures, too.

GLORIA
People are constantly asking for autographs for another person, as if trying to destroy the suspicion that they are actually for themselves. What's your name, Lieutenant?

NICK
Slick trick, Lieutenant. His name is Patrick. Everyone calls him Pattie.

GLORIA smiles coquettishly, signs the notepad and gives it back to the Lieutenant.

BRIAN
Can we get on with things here?

SHELDON
Why rush? It's not like Chet's going to get any deader.

GLORIA
Chet. My dear, sweet Chet. Such talent. Such heart. I can't believe he's gone.

SHELDON
Are we talking about the same man?

BRIAN
The one who stole your diary during one of your clandestine dalliances?

LT. CALLAHAN
Diary?

NORA
We don't know that. It was found in his breast pocket, right?

NICK
Yes. What do you know, Nancy Drew?

NORA
I know he hasn't left this area since we got here. I know he hugged me. You saw that, Nicky.

NICK
I did.

NORA
Well, I certainly would have felt a hard cover book in his breast pocket. And I didn't. That could only mean–

NICK
Someone must have placed it there after his death. Oh, you are a clever little bunny.

NORA
I learned from the best.

LT. CALLAHAN
Quiet down, everyone.

BRIAN
No offense, Lieutenant, but maybe Mrs. Charles is mistaken. Or maybe she's lying to protect his image. Chet spoke often about "the one that got away." That was you, wasn't it, Nora?

NORA
Oh, that was eons ago.

NICK
If Mrs. Charles says she felt nothing, I can assure you, she is correct. She has become expert in noticing an unusual bulge in clothing. Her fashion sense is beyond reproach.

NORA
Thank you, darling.

LT. CALLAHAN
Hold the phone here. I am in charge now. With all this jabbering, I can't think. I am afraid, you'll have to hand over that diary, Miss Wray.

GLORIA
No. I can't. It's private. Mr. Charles...

NICK
If I may.

NICK carefully handles the diary with his handkerchief.

NICK
Lt. Callahan, surely you don't need the whole diary. The front and back cover should be enough. Whoever handled it would have surely left their fingerprints on the spine of the book while placing it on the body. I removed the book carefully, so the only fingerprints that would be natural would be Miss Wray's of course.

LT. CALLAHAN
Yes. I suppose that would be alright.

NICK
I am sorry to destroy your property, Miss Wray, but I shall see to it that these pages remain safe with me.

NICK begins to tear the diary.

BRIAN
Wait.

Everyone freezes.

BRIAN
Ok, you're going to find my fingerprints on that diary. But I didn't kill him. I swear!

GLORIA
What were you doing with my diary? How could you possibly–

NICK
I thought as much. You were one of a select few able to obtain access to Miss Wray's hotel room. In fact, you were the only one who could have possibly ransacked Miss Wray's room to make it look like a robbery. You are used to dressing sets.

BRIAN
You are good, Mr. Charles. Just like I remembered. But I ain't copping to murder. How'd you figure it?

NICK
You were late two days in a row. Bad form for a stage manager! You had Chester's medication both days. You had the key to Madeline's apartment. You could have slipped the diary on Chet any time. You were the first to find his body. My only question is —¬†why do it?

LT. CALLAHAN
Yes. Exactly my question. Why?

BRIAN
It's complicated. I wouldn't... I couldn't kill him. I... I loved him.

SHELDON
Well, butter my butt and call me a biscuit! Whad'ya know?

BRIAN
Oh, don't look so shocked. You think I stayed with this company because of the accolades? The rave reviews? Ha! Actors are a buncha babies. It was Chester. We had a good thing going. Real good. Until SHE came along. Chester was so desperate to get his play produced, he would have done anything or anyone. And Gloria was so accommodating. He played her like a fiddle to get the backing. He milked her like the cash cow she is. Yeah, I took the diary. Chet told me where she kept it, and I tossed the joint to throw suspicion off him. They were always together, you see. I wasn't really going to blackmail her. I just wanted to scare her. I figured she'd quit the show. I mean, who has $5000 dollars these days? It was a ridiculous amount. I just wanted her gone. Then things could go back to the way they were. I'm sorry, Gloria. Love makes people do crazy things. You oughta know.

NICK
Blackmail is still blackmail, whatever the outcome. Right, Lieutenant?

LT. CALLAHAN
Yes, Nick. Blackmail and attempted extortion are still felonies. I gotta take you in, Mr. Talbot. And Nick, I think you need to take up another hobby.

NICK
I tried running, but the ice kept falling out of my glass.

BRIAN
(pointing at ANYA)
I know I did wrong, But she's the one who probably killed him. Where did that peanut come from? Everyone knew Chet was highly allergic.

ANYA
(gasping)
Maybe it was me.

NORA
Oh, don't be silly dear.

ANYA
No, I don't mean it was me who put it in the glass, but every morning I walk through Central Park. It's so lovely. I always grab a handful of shelled peanuts to feed the squirrels. But I always wash my hands and I... oh no... I never threw out...

ANYA runs and gets her coat. She takes out a handful of shelled peanuts. She sighs with relief. It looks as if they are all in their shells until she sees one broken open with one peanut missing.

ANYA
Oh no! I would never.

NORA
Of course she wouldn't, Lieutenant. This is her first professional job, why would she want to jeopardize that?

LT. CALLAHAN
That's exactly what I intend to find out. Now, Miss...

ANYA
Ranevskya. Anya Ranevskya.

SHELDON
Shoulda changed that name.

LT. CALLAHAN
A foreigner, huh? We don't take kindly to foreigners in these parts.

NICK
What is this, the wild west?

LT. CALLAHAN
Can't be too careful these days. Ever hear of Mata Hari? What brings you to the big city, little lady?

ANYA
Nick and Nora. I came with them, after they solved the Cherry Orchard Murder.

LT. CALLAHAN
Right. Now I recall. A murder involving your own family, wasn't it, Mrs Charles?

NORA
Yes. A murder Nick solved while the police were busy suspecting the wrong person. You're on the wrong track here, Lieutenant.

LT. CALLAHAN
And just how did you come to be so connected to the Charleses, Miss... Ranes... Ranev...

ANYA
Anya. My sister is married to Nora's cousin, Simon. After the... incident... I couldn't stay in Moscow anymore. All I ever wanted to be was an actress. But in Russia, studying with Stanislavski was impossible. Nick and Nora have been so good to me. I stayed with them until I started waitressing and making my own living. I live at the Barbizon Hotel for women now. Honestly, I've never been in any trouble. I am studying hard, Mr. Lieutenant, sir. Nora is my sponsor. I owe them so much.

NORA
Anya is practically family.

NICK
Not exactly a ringing endorsement, if you know the Forrest family, but no murderers, Lieutenant. I proved that. Our Anya is as American as apple pie.

LT. CALLAHAN
Ha! Gotcha there, Mr. Charles. Apple pie ain't originally American. It's European. Just like our little missy here. I'm afraid I am going to have to take you down to the station house for further questioning.

ANYA
But I... I didn't do anything. Nick...

NORA
Oh, Pattie, don't be ridiculous. Our Anya was traumatized by her last boyfriend. Held her at gunpoint.

LT. CALLAHAN
An experience like that might cause a person to become unhinged. Ever hear of "Jolly Jane?" Face like an angel. Killed 31 people. Nope. I'm not taking any chances with the Russki.

ANYA
Please! I would never–

NICK
Go with the man, Anya. If the murderer is still among us, you are probably safer in jail.

GLORIA
Wait! What if I drop the charges on Mr. Talbot?

LT. CALLAHAN
Why on earth would you want to do that?

GLORIA
Actors are a dime-a-dozen, but good stage managers are worth their weight in gold!

LT. CALLAHAN
A murder has been committed, Miss Wray. I am afraid it's curtains for this little play of yours. Come on, you two. Since this is a church, I will refrain from using my handcuffs, but don't try anything funny.

ANYA looks pleadingly at NICK as she exits with BRIAN and LT. CALLAHAN.

NORA
Oh Nick. What are we going to do?

NICK
I believe I am going to have a good stiff drink.

NICK pulls out his flask.

NICK
Who's with me?

NICK passes the flask around. Everyone takes a good long swig as the lights fade.

BLACKOUT

END OF ACT ONE

ACT 2, SCENE 1

NICK and NORA's NYC apartment. They are in their pajamas if a change is possible, having some breakfast in the living room. NICK is mildly hung over and resting on the couch. NORA is reading the morning papers. NICK is reading the script.

NORA
Nicky, this is terrible.

NICK
I wouldn't say terrible. Stodgy perhaps, rather passé, but it's a moot point. I am sorry your theatrical debut was cut short, my dove. You were quite fetching on stage. In fact, I'd like to fetch you right now!

NORA
Not the play. The papers. Have you seen them?

NICK
Never before breakfast. Harsh truths in the morning are hard on the digestion. Where'd you get those, anyway?

NORA
Mr. Gordon in 2A works the graveyard shift. Sleeps in. Listen to this. "A final scene was played out in a small Manhattan production this weekend. Silent screen star Gloria Wray's comeback was silenced, after the mysterious death of amateur director Chester McNeill." Oh, Chet would have hated that!

NICK
Yes. Didn't even make the front page. Darn you, Orson Welles, and your radio play hoax!

NORA
No mention of you either, my darling.

NICK
Obviously, a substandard fish wrapper. Kindly return that to Mr. Gordon.

NORA folds up the paper. The doorbell rings. Thinking they are busted, NORA hides the paper. Doorbell rings again.

NICK
Who in the world would be calling on us at this ridiculous hour?

NORA
Well, it is after noon, dear.

NICK
If it's Mr. Gordon, tell him our doorman is a drunk. If it's our liquor delivery, have him bring it straight into the bedroom.

There is barking from off stage.

NICK
Clearly, Asta does not wish to be disturbed. Let sleeping dogs lie, and their owners as well.

Doorbell rings again.

NORA
Hand me my purse, dear. If it's the delivery boy, he'll want a big tip. Mondays are our largest order.

NICK tosses NORA her purse, she grabs some change and the paper and crosses to the door. She checks the peephole and opens the door. GLORIA sweeps in.

NORA
Nicky...

GLORIA
I came right over after I read the morning paper.

NICK staggers back out, obviously disappointed it wasn't the delivery boy.

NORA
Awful, isn't it?

GLORIA
(Ignores NORA, goes straight to NICK)
Simply awful. Don't you think they should have used a different photo of me? And really– page three? I thought Mr. Hearst knew how to sell papers!

NICK
Disgraceful. Chet should have been more thoughtful and died on a slower news day.

GLORIA
But look here, Mr. Charles. They say my play will be cancelled.

NORA
Have you had breakfast, Miss Wray?

GLORIA
I couldn't possibly think of food at a time like this... Just some toast would be nice.

NORA hands her the breakfast try, and pours her some coffee. During the scene, GLORIA eats everything on the tray.

NICK
Please, sit down.

GLORIA
They can't cancel my play, Mr. Charles. They just can't!

NICK
Well, technically, it's Chet's play. He's the writer and director, and dead, lest we forget.

GLORIA
All the more reason to keep it going! An homage to him. There is no such thing as bad publicity. In this case, anyway. I have invested a lot of time and money in this play. I own the script now.

NICK
Interesting. Do you have that in writing?

GLORIA
It was... an oral agreement.

NORA
(under her breath)
I'll bet.

GLORIA
Point being... The show MUST go on, Mr. Charles.

NICK
And how do you propose we do that? We have no playwright. We have no director.

NORA
And we might have a murderer.

GLORIA
That's why we need YOU, Mr. Charles. YOU can direct it!

NICK
Me? I'm flattered, but I have never even directed traffic.

NORA
You could do it, Nicky. Think of poor Anya.

GLORIA
Who?

NICK
Yes. Anya. I must call Lt. Callahan. See what's happening with the investigation.

GLORIA
Please, Mr. Charles. This would mean so much to me personally. And to my fans. They have been dying to see me.

NICK
That's what I am afraid of.

NORA
And if there is a murder to be solved–

NICK
No. I know better than to usurp another man's investigation. Besides, you told me–

NORA
Yes. No more detecting. But this is our Anya, sitting in the slammer. In no time, she could become a mark to some pennyweight grifter, or worse. We are supposed to be looking out for her. I promised her mother we would keep her safe. Nicky, you have to!

GLORIA
I would consider it a monumental favor to me, personally, Mr. Charles. And of course, I would pay you. It is a Herculean undertaking.

NICK
I shall need an undertaker if the no drinking rule still applies.

GLORIA
Whatever you need, Mr. Charles. Please. Don't let this play die. It's the one thing keeping me alive.

NICK
Yes. We must keep the arts alive. And each other.

NORA
Then you'll do it? Oh, Nicky!

NORA hugs him.

NICK
I need to have a chat with Lt. Callahan, but go ahead, Miss Wray. Gather the troops. If the church is no longer a crime scene, we can proceed.

GLORIA
Godspeed, Mr. Charles!

GLORIA kisses both cheeks.

GLORIA
I shall alert the media.

GLORIA exits. NICK looks at NORA and takes a drink.

NICK
Well, my dear, here's another nice mess you've gotten me into.

NORA kisses him on the cheek after wiping off GLORIA's lipstick. Nick picks up the phone and calls LT. CALLAHAN

NICK
Nick Charles here, for Lt. Callahan. Yes, I'll hold. Pour me a drink, darling, I'm starving.

BLACKOUT

ACT 2, SCENE 2

Back at the theater again. NORA, GLORIA SHELDON and BRIAN are all milling about looking at each other suspiciously.

SHELDON
Honestly, Gloria, do you really think it's prudent to go on with this? Especially with the revelations that have recently come to light?

BRIAN
I don't think it's right that we are even here, standing two feet away from the spot where Chet... I feel very uneasy. I think the play is jinxed. This theater is jinxed. I don't want any part of it.

GLORIA
Listen, buddy, I could still press charges, It's the theater or jail. Take your pick.

BRIAN
I'm thinking.

SHELDON
Seems to me, you're stuck between THE rock, and a hard place. Given my druthers, I'd choose the latter, at least there one has honor among thieves.

BRIAN
OOH! Is the green-eyed monster making an appearance? You had to have known. Were you waiting in the wings as well?

SHELDON
How dare you assume? We have been friends for years. He never once mentioned–

GLORIA
Nor to me. I would have known if Chester was "a little light in the loafers." He was all man with me.

BRIAN
Well, that's one thing we have in common.

NORA
Gentlemen! Miss Wray! Let's behave ourselves. After all, Nicky said–

SHELDON
Yes, where is the great Nick Charles, anyway? Why were we all called down here like a bunch of clay pigeons?

We hear barking from offstage. NICK enters with ASTA on the leash. NICK is wearing jodhpurs, a beret, and is carrying a megaphone. He looks like a caricature of a silent movie director.

NICK
(into the megaphone)
Hello, thespians! Your director has arrived!
(to ASTA)
Easy boy. It's safe to be here now.
(to the stunned crowd)
Sorry I am late, everyone. I popped into the bar next door for... breakfast, and Asta needed some... DOG soup. Also, I picked up a little something special on the way.

ANYA enters.

ANYA
Hi, everyone!

NORA rushes up.

NORA
Oh, my dear sweet child! Are you ok?

ANYA
Perfectly fine. The cell was actually warmer than my bedroom in Russia, and once I was cleared, the lieutenant was actually very nice to me. I guess no one wants to be on the wrong side of Nick Charles.

NORA
He has no wrong side, dear. He's delicious. Especially when he's pickled.

SHELDON
So... what happened?

ANYA
It wasn't the peanut.

GLORIA
Well, that's a relief. Natural causes, then? Poor Chet!

NICK
On the contrary. Sit, Asta. Good boy.

NICK approaches the stage with his megaphone.

NICK
Anya is correct. It wasn't the peanut that killed him. He hadn't even touched the glass containing the peanut.

BRIAN
So.... What?

NICK
The ice.

SHELDON
He choked on ice? Surely, we would have heard.

NICK
He didn't choke. The ice was poisoned.

Everyone gasps!

NICK
Yes. Someone put just a drop of arsenic in the ice. He chewed them like mad, and as the ice dissolved in his body...

BRIAN
What a mean way to die.

NICK
Know any nice ways?

GLORIA
That means–

NICK
Yes. One of us in this room is a murderer!

ASTA barks from off stage.

NICK
Sorry, old boy. Not you. No opposable thumbs. So, I doubt very much anyone here wants to continue with our little production.

GLORIA
But we must! I alerted the media! The press alone caused a huge boost in ticket sales. I am doing a radio interview tomorrow. My old Hollywood community has given me their full support.

SHELDON
Really? Are any of them still alive?

GLORIA shoots SHELDON a death glare.

GLORIA
I say damn the torpedos and full speed ahead! If you want to bail, fine. Everyone is replaceable, Mr.Charles. Except me, of course. It's too bad about poor Chet, but is it possible it was suicide?

NICK
Highly doubtful, Miss Wray. Why would a man kill himself slowly in front of everyone, while directing his comeback production?

GLORIA
Who knows why anyone does anything, Mr. Charles? Theater people are a strange bunch. Actually, our little tryst was coming to an end. My husband is due back from Europe for the opening. Many a man has offed himself over me. Chet wouldn't be the first.

LT. CALLAHAN enters.

LT. CALLAHAN
And was that information contained in the pages of that diary, Miss Wray?

NICK
Ah. Lieutenant! I thought you might show up.

LT. CALLAHAN
Nice outfit, Nick. Very becoming.

NICK
Yes. I am becoming thirsty again. Care for a drink, Lieutenant?

LT. CALLAHAN
Very funny. You know the reality. I can't drink on duty.

NICK
Reality is an illusion that occurs due to the lack of alcohol. We're just getting started here. Did you ever consider a career in the arts, Lieutenant? There may be a spot opening up soon.

LT. CALLAHAN
If I wanted to be poor and starving, I would have stayed married to my first wife. She dressed to kill and cooked the same way. Can we get down to business, please?

NICK
Ah. But it's the hungry dog that hunts the best. Don't you think, Lieutenant?

LT. CALLAHAN
Let's cut the banter, Nick. I have a murder to solve here, and no one is above suspicion. Not even you, Nick. I know your wife used to be involved with Mr. McNeill. Maybe you needed to protect your investment. Maybe you were all too happy to top up those ice cubes with a little arsenic.

NORA
Oh, don't be ridiculous. Nicky wasn't ever backstage. He doesn't even drink water.

NICK
Why would I? I've seen what fish do in it.

ANYA
Nick didn't know anything about this play until I told him. If he was so jealous, he could have just told Nora not to do it.

NICK
I have learned never to tell my wife NOT to do anything. That's a guarantee she'll do it over and over again, and probably have photos.

GLORIA
Well, what are we supposed to do? The show opens in two weeks.

LT. CALLAHAN
I do not have the authority to close this production, though I would if I could. What I can insist on is that none of you leave town. You all

LT. CALLAHAN (cont'd)
remain suspects, and you can be assured I will do a very thorough investigation.

NORA
I am sure Nicky could clear this up very quickly, if you gave him half a chance.

LT. CALLAHAN
That would not be prudent, as I have not eliminated you as a suspect, my dear Mrs. Charles.

NORA
Oh, Pattie, you've known us for years!

NICK
Ah, but who really knows what evil lurks behind those bonny brown eyes? Don't worry, my darling, I shall visit you every week if they cart you away, and I promise I will leave enough money in your prison account for the good toilet paper.

LT. CALLAHAN
Look, I ain't sayin' stay out of things. I know you've had some dumb luck nailing goons in the past.

NICK
Yeah, for a dumb guy from Sycamore Springs, I've done alright.

LT. CALLAHAN
Just sayin', if you find out any information, come to me first. Don't be a hero. I seem to recall you've narrowly escaped death a few times.

NICK
Now I'm doing theater, where death is always possible. Stick around, Pattie. I'm about to take my first crack at directing.

LT. CALLAHAN
You all are planning to go ahead with this?

Everyone ad-libs. "Yes. Of course. For the time being, etc".

LT. CALLAHAN
Fine. Break a leg, don't leave town. Nick, you know where to find me.

NICK
And if I'm not here, you know where to find me.

LT. CALLAHAN turns and leaves.

ANYA
Bye! Nice meeting you!

Everyone looks at ANYA like she has three heads.

ANYA
What? I happen to like bread and water.

NICK grabs his megaphone.

NICK
Alright, everyone. Center stage, please. We are going to try something different.

SHELDON
Rehearsing, maybe?

BRIAN
Well, you certainly don't need me. Anyone want some ice water? Oops... Sorry.

NICK
I need everyone. There has been a lot of accusations flying. If we are going to do this play, we need to be unified. A family.

BRIAN
Hopefully not Lizzie Borden's family.

GLORIA
With all due respect, Mr. Charles, I am above silly parlor games.

ANYA
I'm not!

SHELDON
Quelle surprise.

NICK
I think you all will find this useful. I have named it–
(into the megaphone)
"TACTICS." Here's how it works.

BRIAN
Can you put down your "meglamaniaphone," Mr. Charles? We are standing right here.

NICK
Certainly.

NICK takes out his flask, takes a long drink and places it inside the megaphone.

GLORIA
Is that really necessary, Mr. Charles?

NICK
I did not come here to stay sober, Madam. All this excitement has put me behind in my drinking. Gather around. Form a circle. Here are the rules. I will give you a line from the play, and you will throw it around like a football to each other randomly, but each time try to say it with a different tactic. With passion, sadness, suspicion... You get the idea. Your first line is, "I don't want to talk about it."

NICK (cont'd)
(Into the megaphone, taking a swig from the flask inside)
Go!

Everyone is silent, looking at each other. No one is enthusiastic but ANYA.

SHELDON
How about we let Shirley Temple start?

ANYA
Hurray!

ANYA says the line to NORA, NORA to BRIAN, BRIAN To SHELDON, SHELDON to GLORIA, GLORIA (very dramatically) to NORA, who is a little taken aback and looks at NICK.

NICK
Great start.

GLORIA
Are we done? Honestly, Mr. Charles, This newfangled method is irrelevant. Wally Beery and I made 4 films together. You know what our motivation was? Our paycheck.

NICK
Let's just try one more.
(into the megaphone after taking another swig from the flask)
Your line is, "I love you."

ANYA
(to NORA)
I love you.

NORA to BRIAN, BRIAN to ANYA, ANYA to SHELDON, SHELDON to Gloria, GLORIA back to SHELDON. SHELDON and GLORIA go back and forth a few times, broken by...

SHELDON
(to GLORIA, French for "My God! This is ridiculous! I love you!")
Mon dieu! C'est ridicule! Je t'aime! I love you.

GLORIA looks shocked.

NORA
Oh, Nicky, he speaks French. How romantic!

GLORIA
I knew it. I knew it was you. Your face might have changed, but those eyes. STEVE! When you didn't respond to my note, I thought I might be mistaken! Oh, Steve.. Why?

ANYA
(confused)
What page are we on?

NICK
I think I know. Sometimes when you put two and two together, you get four. In this case it's 22.

SHELDON
YOU wrote that note? I figured it was Chester. I figured maybe you talked in your sleep, Gloria. A lot of secrets get revealed in the heat of passion. I figured Chet figured out who I really was.

BRIAN
That's a lot of figuring. Who the hell are you?

GLORIA
This is Steve. Steve Grayson, My second husband.

Everyone reacts with surprise except NICK, who seems to have known already. He pours himself a drink.

NICK
Everyone, have a seat. Take 10.

ANYA
Thank you, 10.

Everyone except NORA groans, tells her to shut up, etc...

GLORIA
You vanished after the death of Walter.
(to everyone)
Walter was my third husband. Do you have any idea what I went through because of the scandal?

NORA
We know, dear. It was all over the papers.

SHELDON
(to NICK)
Gloria collected husbands like squirrels gather nuts for the winter. I tried hard, but all through the marriage she treated me like second hand furniture. Her star was shining, and I was a mere day player. When Walter came on the scene, I was thrown away like yesterday's newspaper. Gloria kept all the rings, and threw away the grooms. She broke my heart. So, I fled to Switzerland. I changed my name. Dyed my hair. Got a nose job. Shaved my beard and lost 20 pounds, grieving over Gloria. Maybe I should have come back for the trial. Maybe I could have helped. But I knew she would be acquitted. There was no real proof, and with her money, she could afford the best lawyers. Money can't buy you happiness, but I took comfort in that it bought Gloria her own form of misery. How many more husbands? Three? Four? Hard to keep track. There is no warm person underneath, Mr. Charles. Beneath her cold exterior, there is just ice water. Ice water in the veins.

NICK
Yet, you returned.

SHELDON
Yes. I came back. I got tired of chocolate and cuckoo clocks. And my settlement only went so far. Chester didn't ask questions. He thought he was the next Noel Coward, and he was happy to be building a company. Me, and then Brian, I had no idea why Brian stuck it out, the plays weren't very good and the pay was worse. Now I know.

BRIAN
So, you should know I wouldn't do anything to hurt him. I guess you know what it's like to hide in the shadows, and to be tossed aside. Another casualty of Gloria Wray.

SHELDON
(to NICK)
When Chet told me the great Gloria Wray approached him about "The Regret of the Danbury Lilly," you could have knocked me over with a feather. With Gloria, this play would have a chance, he said, and we all were going to be paid... a decent salary. I didn't think she'd recognize me, not after all this time and all the changes. I was looking forward to telling her, but just like that, she's involved with Chester. Chet was my friend, but it didn't take long for Gloria to sink her hooks in him. Maybe she even convinced him to blackmail me.

GLORIA
Who would blackmail you? You never had two nickels to rub together. And you got me all wrong, Steve. That note was not a threat. "I know who you are and what you did." You stupid fool. I was forgiving you.

SHELDON
You mean...

GLORIA
Yes. I knew. I was angry that you ran, leaving me to deal with the scandal, but like ice, anger melts away in time.

SHELDON
Gloria...

SHELDON goes to hug her.

SHELDON
I'm so sorry.

NORA
Oh, Nicky. Isn't this sweet?

ANYA
I'm so confused. Is this part of the game?

NICK
We're playing a new game now. It's called True Confessions.

NORA
(to ANYA)
It's like toasting a marshmallow, dear.

ANYA
Huh? We didn't toast marshmallows in Russia. I tried it once over your stove and burnt it to a crisp.

NORA
That's just it. Gloria and Sheldon were so burnt on the outside, they couldn't appreciate how sweet the inside was.

NICK
And sticky. Very sticky. There was something else in the pages of that diary, wasn't there, Miss Wray? Something about that scandal.

GLORIA
Don't make me say it, Mr. Charles. Not now. Walter was a swine.

NICK
A wealthy swine. Spent half his fortune on alcohol, gambling and women. The other half he wasted.

SHELDON
He was a beast. Gloria. How long have you known?

GLORIA
Who else could it have been? You never gave back my key.

ANYA
What's going on?

GLORIA
(to SHELDON)
I never told. I knew you did it for me. I even tried to find you after it was all over. I thought Mexico, but no soap.

ANYA
What am I missing?

BRIAN
Boy, you are naive, aren't you? Sheldon killed Gloria's third husband!

ANYA gasps.

SHELDON
Steve did. But Steve is gone now. Nobody knows but you.

NICK
There is no statute of limitations on murder, Mr. Grayson. Gloria might be willing to forgive and forget. After all, one might say you are a changed man. But some habits die hard. Murder is never perfect. It begins to come apart at the seams, like a cheap Christmas sweater.

GLORIA
Oh, Steve. You didn't.

SHELDON runs and grabs ANYA by the neck! He takes a gun out of his pocket.

ANYA
Oh, no. Not again!

SHELDON
OK. Yeah. I killed Chet. But it was an accident, see? I thought the note was from him, that he was going to give me up.

NICK
If you had known the note was from Gloria, would you have poisoned HER to save yourself?

SHELDON
No. Never. I loved her. I have always loved her. Even if she wrote about it in her diary, it would have implicated Steve, not Sheldon Stuart. Gloria and Chet were the only ones who could have made that connection.

NICK
Unless forensics matched your fingerprints with Steve Grayson's. Lt. Callahan has the bottle, the glasses and the ice cube tray. He will find our fingerprints everywhere, but he won't find Sheldon Stuart's, because Sheldon Stuart doesn't exist. Now I suggest you put down the gun and let Anya go.

SHELDON
Why should I? The penalty for one murder is the same as two or even three. I got nothing to lose. Now back up everyone.

BRIAN backs up towards the lighting board. He turns out the lights. In the blackout, we hear a scuffle, a fight, furniture being turned over, and a gunshot!

NORA
Nicky! Nicky, the lights! By the back wall.

NICK flicks on the lights. Everyone is in a tangle. BRIAN has a gun on SHELDON.

GLORIA
I told you! A good stage manager is worth their weight in gold!

BRIAN
I know this set like the back of my hand.

NICK
Thank you, Brian. I'll take it from here. Would you mind turning up the house lights, as well? Nora, dear, would you kindly run next door to phone Lt. Callahan? And get me a bottle of scotch while you're at it. We're out.

NICK takes the gun from BRIAN and holds it on SHELDON. BRIAN exits, and turns on all lights.

NORA
Oh, Nicky, you are clever.

ANYA
Mind if I come along? I think I can use a drink.

NORA
I must teach you not to stand in close proximity to murderers.

ANYA
And you wonder why I don't date!

NORA and ANYA exit.

BLACKOUT

ACT 2, SCENE 3

LT. CALLAHAN has returned. He is putting handcuffs on SHELDON. Everyone has gathered.

LT. CALLAHAN
I thought I told you not to be a hero, Nick.

NICK
I just kept em talking, Pattie, it's what actors do best. Give em enough rope... and they'll make macrame!

LT. CALLAHAN
I would love to study your brain sometime. Pickled, in a museum.

NORA
He does his best work that way.

NICK hands over the weapon.

NICK
Here's the weapon, Lieutenant. It was recently fired, but luckily no one got hurt, except my flask. Damn bullet went right through it. Luckily, it was empty. Adding the cost of another to the budget.

LT. CALLAHAN
I always knew guns and alcohol don't mix. How much have you had today, Nick?

NORA
Oh, it only takes one drink to get Nick drunk. I just can't remember if it's number 13 or 14.

SHELDON
Let's just get this over with. I did the world a favor, twice. Saved you from that no-good rat of a husband, Gloria, and saved the world of

SHELDON (cont'd)
theater from further McNeill catastrophes! Gloria, my darling, can you get me a good lawyer? I'm sure you must have married one or two.

GLORIA
You're tootin' the wrong ringer, baby. The first one I could forgive, but this? You sabotaged my comeback, Steve. I hope you fry! Get this sap outta my sight, Lieutenant! Oh, Nick, the play... What are we going to do? We are already sold out for opening night!

BRIAN
We are?

GLORIA
I told you there was no such thing as bad publicity! A murder does wonders to boost ticket sales. But who can we get to play Reginald?

NORA
Don't worry, Nicky knows lots of people in low places. What about that waiter?

NICK
Sticky? I almost forgot about him.

GLORIA
I am NOT co-starring with a man named Sticky. Couldn't you do it, Mr. Charles?

NICK
I could, but I prefer to relay directions, not take them. How about you, Pattie? Have you ever considered a career in the arts?

SHELDON
Oh, come on! Don't be ridiculous. You can't just replace me with... some dizzy copper! I worked with Sam Taylor, Victor Sjostrom!

LT. CALLAHAN
Hey, I ain't dizzy, but you are gonna be in a minute!

LT. CALLAHAN raises a hand to hit him with the gun, but NORA stops him.

NORA
Come on, Pattie. You've got a great face. I bet there's an actor inside there. It's a lot safer than police work.

NICK
I wouldn't be to sure about that.

LT. CALLAHAN
Well, I must say... When I performed "Tumbling Tumbleweeds" at the police academy, I pretty much brought the house down. And to work alongside the great Gloria Wray... Well, it would be an honor.

NICK
It's settled, then.

ANYA
Yay!

NICK
Go throw that lousy chump in the clink and let's get to work.

NICK grabs his megaphone.

NICK
See you in the funny papers Shel.. I mean Steve. ABYSSINIA! ("I'll be seein' ya," slang-like)

LT. CALLAHAN starts to exit with SHELDON. ANYA approaches him.

ANYA
May I, Lieutenant?

LT. CALLAHAN gives her the go-ahead. ANYA kicks SHELDON in the shin.

ANYA
I'm sick of men holding guns on me. I'm an actress, not a doormat. That was just mean.

BRIAN
(to SHELDON)
And you've always been a second-rate actor, too.

SHELDON
(to BRIAN)
Now, that hurts!
(to ANYA)
Sorry, little lady. It wasn't personal. Just a "tactic." Nice going, Mr. Charles. Bye, Gloria. Maybe you'll be ready for husband number nine, if I don't end up doin' a dance at the end of a rope. Dyin' won't be hard, Lieutenant. I've been dead for years... It's comedy that's tough!

LT. CALLAHAN leads SHELDON away.

ANYA
Wow.

GLORIA
Gotta hand it to him. That was a pretty good exit line.

NICK picks up his megaphone, which might have a big bullet hole in it, which would distort the sound. Nick puts his finger over the hole.

NICK
Take it from the top ladies and, oh... Brian... You still in?

BRIAN
I'm in. Places, everyone!

NICK
(into his megaphone)
"The Regret of the Danbury Lilly." Scene ONE!

The actors begin to scramble to their places as BRIAN fixes the upturned chairs and the lights fade.

BLACKOUT

ACT 2, SCENE 4

Two weeks later. NICK and NORA's apartment. Everyone has gathered. They are nervous, excited. NICK has a bottle of champagne.

NORA
How are you feeling?

NICK
Awful, I went to bed sober.

NICK goes to open the bottle of champagne.

NORA
You can't open it yet, Nicky. It's bad luck.

NICK
Either way I will need a drink.
(Pause)
Fine.

He takes a drink from his new flask.

GLORIA
What is keeping Anya?

NORA
Nicky, you really shouldn't have sent that poor girl out alone. Trouble does seem to follow her.

NICK
She's not alone. Asta is with her. Besides, she volunteered to get the morning edition.

BRIAN
I still can't believe George F. Kaufman wrote us a review.

GLORIA
Surely, that will bring Mr. Griffith in from California.

LT. CALLAHAN
If it's a good one.

NORA
You did a wonderful job, Pattie.

BRIAN
Yeah, but I wouldn't give up my day job if I were you. The theater is a fickle business.

ANYA is heard offstage.

ANYA
No! Bad dog! No, Asta! Give that back! Oh, nuts... That was the last copy.

NORA opens the door. ANYA runs in with ASTA on the leash. He is running ahead of her with the paper in his mouth. ASTA runs into the bedroom. (This can be imagined/mimed, etc.)

ANYA
Nick, I'm so sorry. He just grabbed the paper.

NICK
I'll get it.

NICK walks into the bedroom. We hear some growling. NICK walks out with a shredded newspaper.

NICK
Everyone's a critic.

NORA
I'll go see if Mr. Gordon in 2A has his.

NORA runs out. She comes back with another shredded newspaper.

NORA
Apparently, Asta is not fond of the Herald Tribune, either.

ANYA
I'm so sorry, Nick. But I'm good at puzzles, I bet we can put this together.

NICK puts the shredded newspaper on the table and they start trying to piece it together.

NICK
Here's one... "Arrived in high style..."

GLORIA
Who? Who?

NICK continues.

NICK
"Spirited. Light hearted comedy."

BRIAN
They thought it was a comedy?

NICK
"Entertainingly clever spoof... whip smart..."

NORA
Look what I found. "Nora Charles, heir to the Forrest steel fortune, debuted in the society pages some years ago..." Oh, I don't think I like this...

ANYA
Wait. Here's the next bit. "Debuted last night in The Regret of the Danbury Lilly, skillfully directed by her husband, former Pinkerton and detective Nick Charles of Thin Man fame..."

NICK takes a drink at the word "former."

NICK
Former?! That's libelous.

ANYA
"The ever-ebullient Nora Charles brought essential femininity and impeccable timing to her role, forever negating the idea that husbands and wives should not work together."

NORA hugs NICK.

NICK
Very astute man, that Mr. Kaufman.

GLORIA
Me. What did he say about me?

NICK
Ah. Yes...

He picks up another scrap.

NICK
"Snappy supporting cast... Steely-eyed Patrick Callahan... handsome and agreeable..." No, not that...

NICK tosses that aside.

LT. CALLAHAN
Hey!

LT. CALLAHAN grabs that slip of paper and puts it into his wallet.

NICK
"Minimalist set, deftly accomplished by Brian...." Oh, here, this must belong to you.

NICK hands the scrap to BRIAN.

NICK
"Anya Ravenskya's..." Hey, they spelled your name right! "....star shone brightly in the role of Lilly. Miss Ranevskya is a suave and polished young actress, and it gives me unmitigated pleasure to introduce her to the theater world."

ANYA
Hot damn!

ANYA grabs her piece, kisses it and puts it close to her heart.

NORA
Your mama will be so proud. Be sure to send our love.

GLORIA
Oh, this is ridiculous!

She grabs the phone.

GLORIA
Give me the number of the New York Times.
(to NICK)
I'm going to hear this review uninterrupted if I have to buy the whole newspaper office.

NICK
No need, it's right here. "Saving the best for last..."

GLORIA
(putting the receiver down)
It's about time. Read on, Mr. Charles.

NICK
"Gloria Wray, undiminished by time, is effervescent and positively regal in the comedic role of Madeline. Miss Wray's ability to parody her silent movie persona, was a definite crowd pleaser. Audiences may have come because of the scandal but they left, treated to a new and transformed side of the exquisite Miss Wray. My prediction is that Danbury Lilly will transfer to Broadway, and will soon rival Hellzapoppin' as the longest running play of 1938."

NORA
We're a hit!

ANYA
Boy howdy!

BRIAN
Oh, Chet. Wherever you are, I hope you are laughing.

NICK
(pouring the champagne)
To Chester McNeill and his accidental hit.

Everyone takes a drink and says "To CHET!"

GLORIA
And to you Mr. Charles, for not giving up on us despite the unexpected turn of events.

NICK
I have always found that the truth, no matter how unpleasant it is, can always lead to libations.

Everyone holds up their drink and says "To Mr. Charles!"

LT. CALLAHAN
Well, Nick, I guess it's a new career for the two of us, huh?

NICK
When the going gets tough, the tough go drinking. Would you like something a little stronger than champagne?

LT. CALLAHAN
I believe I would.

NICK pours them both a healthy scotch from the bar. There is a constant ringing of the doorbell.

NORA
Now who could that be?

BRIAN
They certainly are persistent.

GLORIA
It might be my husband. He was flying back from Europe today.

NICK
Then he should be resting his fingers. Hold on. I'm coming.

NICK opens the door. A strange man is standing there. It is the same actor as CHESTER, but looks radically different to not confuse anyone.

MAN
Mr. Charles, I need your help. The play.... Gloria Wray...... I have... ACK....

He falls down dead, with a knife in his back! GLORIA and ANYA scream! NICK quickly looks down the hall, and sees no one.

NORA
Nicky, who is this man?

NICK
Not sure, he just dropped in.
(turns him over)
Wait, this is Sticky's brother. I didn't figure him for a fan of the theater.

LT. CALLAHAN
(Approaching the body)
Anyone know what he might have been doing here?

They all shake their heads.

LT. CALLAHAN
Well, Nick, looks like we are going to be doing double-duty for a while. May I?

Nick gestures to the phone.

LT. CALLAHAN
Captain Abrams, please. Yeah. We got an egg here in need of a Chicago overcoat. Send the wagon to the Charles's place. Second Floor.

NICK starts pouring drinks for everyone. They are standing there in shock. Nobody drinks except NICK. LT. CALLAHAN covers the body with a blanket.

NICK
Mrs. Charles?

NORA
Well, here we go again!

NICK and NORA clink their glasses and drink while everyone else stands there frozen in shock.

**LIGHTS FADE
END OF PLAY**

We always like to add a little extra amusement for the audience (and the cast!), especially when a play is in its early stages. We made these pictures in Photoshop for the first reading, to help create the atmosphere of the play-within-the-play.

More plays by Bambi Everson

Visit BambiEverson.com

Also available in paperback

THE THIN MAN IN THE CHERRY ORCHARD

In this sardonic mashup, Dashiell Hammett's hard-boiled, glamorously pickled American sleuths, Nick and Nora Charles, meet their cousins, the stoic inhabitants of Chekhov's bleak Russian tundra. Naturally, a murder, and hilarity, ensues. Can Nick solve the crime before they run out of vodka? Full length, approximately 100 minutes, one optional intermission. Comedy-Mystery. 4M, 4F.

Also available in paperback

FINDING ANDREW
Twelve-year-old Virginia's peculiar connection to Andrew is met with uncertainty and doubt by her best friend, Max. One act, approximately 22 minutes. Drama. 1F, 2 teens (M/F)

DAD'S HOME
Paul is home from the office. Something is terribly wrong, and everybody knows but him. One act, approximately 50 minutes. Drama. 2M, 1F, 1M teen.

Also available in paperback

SINCERELY HELD BELIEFS

Mandy is caught between her two friends. One a grieving mother, and the other a zealous clairvoyant who is convinced she is receiving messages from the other side. Mandy must try to mediate these two relationships, while staying true to her own beliefs. Full length, approximately 80 minutes. Psychological Drama 3F, 20s-40s. Trigger warning: child death.

Also available in paperback

NEITHER HERE NOIR THERE
Michael, newly divorced, has taken up residence with his best friend, Alice. He begins to rework a discarded film noir novel, but soon his femme fatale, Maxie Malone, comes to life with an agenda of her. *Blithe Spirit* meets *The Maltese Falcon*. Full length, approx. 60 minutes. Comedy. 2F, 1M.

UNPLUGGED
A writer's work is disrupted when his printer takes on a life, and an agenda, of its own. One act, approx. 50 minutes. Dark comedy. 2F, 2M.

Also available in paperback

MURDER IS SERVED
A murderous love triangle amongst octogenarians in an assisted living facility. Married for 40 years, Steve Lowenthal's life has been made intolerable by his henpecking wife, Rita. Finding new love in the rehabilitation center leads to deceit, treachery, revenge and cheating at Scrabble. One act, approx. 45 minutes. Dark Comedy. 2F, 2M.

DECEPTION
A brief encounter in a bar leads to a complicated entanglement. Dishonesty and lying are rampant, but who is doing what? One act, approx. 55 minutes. Drama/Mystery. 2F, 2M.

Bambi Everson

ABOUT THE AUTHOR

Bambi Everson is a playwright, actor, and teaching artist. Her full-length, THE THIN MAN IN THE CHERRY ORCHARD had a sold out run at the 2019 New York Fringe Festival, and is among a growing series of her plays available in paperback from The Drama Book Shop and Amazon. Her work has also been produced at Manhattan Repertory Theatre, Hudson Guild, Emerging Artists Theatre, The Little Theatre of Alexandria, VA, and college productions in North Carolina and Arkansas.

She studied with Geraldine Page and Michael Schulman, and appeared in many Off-Off Broadway productions in her youth. She wrote her first play in 2015, and has since completed over 30 more, including six full lengths.

Her work tends to incorporate oddball characters and situations. Subject matter has ranged from screwball comedy to dark melodrama, from cannibals in suburban Long Island, to blind dates with bearded ladies. She's been influenced as much by cinema as she has by theater, an inescapable accident of birth, as she's the daughter of noted film historian, William K. Everson.

She was the recipient of the 2015 Yip Harburg Foundation award. She teaches playwriting in Manhattan, and is a member of Actors' Equity and The Dramatist's Guild.

Follow her adventures at her website, bambieverson.com

www.ingramcontent.com/pod-product-compliance
Lightning Source LLC
LaVergne TN
LVHW051844080426
835512LV00018B/3067